Words Pressed into Seams

Ruby F. Nazaruk

Books by Ruby F. Nazaruk

Story Collections

Words In All Their Splendor
A String Called Love
A Journey of People & Ourselves
Do You Have a Pen?
A Trail of What if's & Love
The Author's Mind
Bedtime Stories for Children
Leaves & their Whispers
Soul's Intertwined
The Bizarre & Strange Story Collection
The Heart of Paradise
Unspoken: A Collection of Words Left Unsaid
Waves & Their Secrets
Cabin Fever

Ruby's Faith Collection

God Instances

A Journey with Our Lady

God's Call

Ruby's Learning Collection

Living Life with Dyslexia

The Rain Travelers

Where The Rain Takes You

Stand-Alone Novels

Lost Eyes

Words Pressed into Seams

RUBY F. NAZARUK

ISBN: 978-1-7383590-4-2

DEDICATION

I dedicate this book to the history of me, for those who have shaped me.

CONTENTS

ACKNOWLEDGMENTS

I really enjoyed creating this story collection.
A big thank you to all those who continue to support and encourage me.
For my family and friends.

1 QUILTED STORY

A quilted story
Words sewn together
Stories
The fabric of life
The fabric moves and is alive
The thread of time
Words pressed into seams
Squares and scraps
The story of a quilt
A Patchwork Quilt's Tale
Patterns and colors galore
Measure twice, cut once, unless you are dyslexic and your math gets confused, then measure triple the times.
Threads of fate
A quilt's tale
Generations of quilters, sewists, and artist-creators who paint in squares of fabric

2 IN ONE'S BLOOD

My name is Ruby, and this is my story. Well, I suppose it's other people's stories. Stories of generations and blood running through one's veins.

Short story on literature. I like to say that creativity runs through my veins. My love of books and literature grew with every bedtime story and all those books my parents read to my siblings and me. I remember nights when our mother or father read *Little House on the Prairie* out loud to us before bed.

Our mother sang us songs, read us books, and left recordings for us whenever she was away.

My great-great-grandmother, Nancekevill, was one of the first librarians at the Athabasca and District Public Library. Founded in 1946 and renamed the Alice B. Donahue Library and Archives, the library opened on January 15, 1947, and is still open to this day. In 1997, the year I was born, the library celebrated its fifty years.

While I never met my grandmother.

Nancekevill, I like to think that she would be proud of me and the writer I have become. That we would have shared our love of reading and books.

The library has always been a magical place for me—word-filled pages and everything waiting to be discovered. Shelves stacked with novels, encyclopedias, poetry, and adventure stories whispered secrets and adventures into the quiet air. I would wander the aisles, running my fingers along the spines, imagining the worlds inside each book.

I loved the smell of old paper, the crispness of new pages, and the gentle hush that seemed to float in the reading rooms. From fairy tales to histories, from dusty tomes to brightly colored children's books, the library was a treasury of imagination. I could spend hours discovering new stories, tracing my fingers over the worn covers of classics, or flipping the pages of books filled with faraway lands, talking animals, and heroes on daring quests.

There were books that smelled of adventure: leather-bound novels with gilded edges, stories of knights, dragons, and princesses. There were books that smelled of wisdom: encyclopedias, reference volumes, and dictionaries where words waited patiently to be uncovered. And there were books that smelled like home: picture books from my childhood, with familiar stories and familiar voices echoing from the pages.

I remember sitting cross-legged on the floor, a book open on my lap, completely absorbed. The world around me faded, replaced by the forests of Narnia, and the small prairie houses of Laura Ingalls. Words became windows, doors, and bridges to other lives, and I felt as if I were walking alongside every character, living their triumphs, learning from their mistakes, and discovering the power of imagination.

Every time I visited the library, I felt a connection to generations of readers before me, to Great-Great Grandma Nancekevill, whose hands had once touched those same shelves; to the children who had scrawled their names inside the front covers of borrowed books; to the librarians who carefully tended the stories like gardeners tending fragile blooms. I was part of something larger than myself. The library was alive, and I was alive within it.

I loved the quiet corners with chairs tucked beside tall shelves, where one could curl up and lose oneself in poetry, philosophy, or a collection of myths. I loved the rolling ladders that reached the highest shelves, daring me to climb and see what treasures awaited above. I loved the tables scattered with open books, where students and dreamers poured over the pages, their pencils scratching notes, their eyes lighting up with discovery.

And as I grew, the library grew with me. The books I read as a child led me to new ones as a teen, which led me to novels as an adult, and then to writing my own stories, inspired by the countless voices that had shaped me. The library was no longer just a place; it was a mentor, a friend, a keeper of history and possibility.

I like to think that creativity runs in our blood because it is nurtured by moments like these: bedtime stories, parents reading aloud, libraries that open their doors to anyone curious enough to enter. My own stories now flow from a lifetime of listening to others, from walking those aisles, from breathing in the scent of paper and ink and imagination. Every page I write is a nod to those who came before me, to the storytellers and librarians, to the family that fostered the love of words and worlds.

The library has always been a magical place for me. Word-filled pages, stories waiting to be discovered, adventures ready to be lived, and wisdom quietly waiting to be understood.

It taught me patience, curiosity, and reverence for the written word.

And as I write, I imagine Nancekevil smiling, proud of the generations of readers and writers who continue to find magic between the covers of a book.

3 DNA

I took my first pottery lessons in the Athabasca Pottery Club—the same place where my great-great-grandmother, Katherine Rypien, did pottery. When I think of all the gifts I was blessed with, sometimes I see the gifts and ties to the family and generations of old. While I never met my great-grandmother, Katherine, I think I would have really liked her.

My favorite pillow as a child was a patchwork one that was in my grandparents' cabin. Grandma Katherine had made it. It always spoke to me. I grew up watching my mother sew and quilt. While I learned to sew, I never really learned to quilt. I learned to knit and many other things. Then I spent some time with my grandmother learning to build a quilt. Quilts can have their own stories and their own meanings. When I think of all the possibilities, the words sewn and pressed into the seams, it makes me smile. For it is much like words stretched out across a page. There are many stories waiting to be told. Some are just waiting to be written, others are for the right audience.

Storytelling has been passed down throughout human history. It has been passed down from generation to generation. There are times when we forget that all stories have to start somewhere, born into existence when somebody takes the time to utter the words into the void of time. Libraries and archives hold history, and sometimes it's in her blood. Being a history major and a writer, I've always been fascinated by archives. I think about my great-grandmother being a librarian. Sometimes it just makes sense that when I was in high school, I became a library page, and I spent a lot of time amongst the shelves, filled with books and stories waiting to be read, discovering the new worlds and things one just might not think of. I found my home amongst the pages, amongst the sounds of pages turning and the smell of old books. There is nothing better than an antique store or a vintage bookstore filled with books. Think of it now: I see it right in front of me, or behind me, awakening me from my past, from generations before me.

Since I was a kid, I've always wanted to be a writer and an author, to share my stories with others besides my brothers. I was told everything else didn't matter—just to begin somewhere, to get it down on paper. So I began writing in my journals and notebooks for as long as I can remember. Writing is natural, like breathing. Sometimes it feels as though my books are writing themselves, and other times I realize all the bits and pieces that were written over time, over the years of my life, all converging into one collection, or another, mixed with the new, brought to life simply by believing that dreams do come true—that if I put my mind to it, I can make it happen.

God has blessed me with the gift of storytelling, the love of creativity and art, and reading books. There's a quote by Marcus Garvey: *"A people without the knowledge of their past history, origin, and culture is like a tree without roots."* Understanding one's past and the generations that live within our DNA, our blood, are reminders of who we are.

4 PARTS OF ME

I love the rain and puddles; I always have to resist jumping in them at inappropriate times. The sound of raindrops on the leaves, the splash of water beneath my boots—these were small joys I never wanted to resist.

I was a tomboy growing up, and mud and dirt never bothered me. The soil was part of life, part of adventure, part of play. Hands and clothes could get messy, but the world felt more real that way, more tangible, more mine.

And yet, I loved musicals and plays. I loved the music, the movement, the stories told through song and dance. There was a rhythm to it that reminded me of life outside the fields—the rhythm of imagination, of creativity, of stepping into someone else's world for a time.

I grew up balancing the wildness of the countryside with the magic of performance, running barefoot through mud and singing to the clouds. Both were part of who I was, shaping me into someone who could find joy in the simplest moments and wonder in the grandest stories.

5 HELPING HAND

As a kid, I had a blue fanny pack. It served as my tool belt. Ever since I was a kid, I've been the one to help Dad keep track of his tools while he works on a project.

Now I'm grown, and I still help him organize and keep track. While I don't have a fanny pack, my pockets always have the tools needed. Tape measure. Pens. Markers. Mini level. I have it. Tell me a tool you need, and I'll hand it to you. I am a handy helper, and I can lend a hand when needed.

The sounds of tinging screws in one's pockets, sparks flashing and flying about as the grinder casts and cuts at metal, the smell of cut plywood—all of it familiar, comforting. The sounds of a whirling drill fill the air, steady and sure.

The smell of cherries, specifically that of car cleaner, lingers faintly—a small, sweet note amid the hum of work.

These are the moments etched in time, simple and steady. The rhythm of creation. The bond between father and child, built in sawdust and sound. Some things never leave you; they only change shape, carried quietly in pockets and memory.

6 AERIAL VIEW

The aerial view was like a patchwork quilt made up of squares and hues as far as the eye could see. It was the kind of view that stirred something deep inside—a quiet ache of memory, a reminder of days gone by.

From above, the land unfolded softly beneath the clouds, each piece stitched together by time and tender care. Fields of gold, ribbons of green, and winding streams shimmered in the sunlight, like threads in a well-loved quilt passed down through generations.

There was a sense of peace in it all, a hush that seemed to whisper of simpler times—of hands that once toiled in those fields, of laughter carried on the breeze, of lives woven gently into the land.

It was beautiful, achingly so. The kind of beauty that tugs at the heart, that makes one long to return, even if only in memory, to stand once more upon that soil and feel the rhythm of life humming quietly beneath one's feet.

7 DIRT ROADS

Dirt roads weaving and winding through
lush green forest,
all around bushes galore,
The sounds of dirt between someone's
tires. Oh, what a lovely day,
Oh, how beautiful it is to be in the
countryside—
Down and wandering, weaving country
roads.
Country roads lead you home;
They lead too far and wide,
Wherever one's heart desires.
Take a stroll, or rather a leisurely drive,
Windows down, wind in your hair,
The sun spilling warmth through the trees.
The scent of earth and pine fills the air,
And the world seems softer here—
Slower, quieter, kinder.
Every turn feels like a memory waiting to
be made,
Every mile is a reminder.
that sometimes the most beautiful
destinations
These are the ones that find you along the
way.

8 MY TEACHER

My mom, a speech adjudicator by trade, is my teacher.

I grew up with the saying: Uncle Walter special. It was a phrase that held weight and warmth, a little piece of family history that we carried with us through everyday life.

My mom's love for speech, poems, and storytelling shaped so much of my childhood.

She loved the rhythm of words, the way a well-chosen phrase could lift a story or a poem to life. Whenever she was away, she'd record cassette tapes with songs and her reading stories so it wouldn't be so hard to be apart.

I would listen to her voice echoing from the tapes, feeling her presence even when she was not physically there.

It was a small comfort, a bridge across the distance, and it made me realize that stories and words could hold people together, even across miles.

Being homeschooled, our mother was

not just our mother but our teacher. She guided our learning, nurtured our creativity, and instilled a love of words and expression that has stayed with me my whole life. Lessons were more than just textbooks and assignments—they were stories, poems, and conversations that shaped the way I saw the world.

Her classroom was our home, and her lessons were threaded into the very fabric of our everyday lives.

My mother was a Concordia alumna, and I was excited to follow in those footsteps. The idea of walking the same halls, learning under the same values, and discovering my own path through the love of words and education felt like a continuation of the legacy she had gifted me.

I imagined her guiding me still, even invisibly, as I explored new ideas, memorized poems, and found my own voice in writing.

Through her love of speech and storytelling, my mother taught me more than reading and writing.

She taught me patience, expression, and the power of words. She showed me that stories are more than just words on a page—they are connections, memories, bridges to others, and echoes of who we are.

And even now, years later, I carry her lessons with me, as though her voice is still reading aloud in the corners of my mind, guiding me, encouraging me, and reminding me of the magic found in every word.

9 MOTHER & ME

You'll always be my mom,
and I know your love
Will never leave me.
I know that you have always tried your best,
and you have always been
my biggest supporter,
The one who lifts me up
when I feel unsure,
The one who believes in me
Even when I doubt myself.
You are mine,
and I am yours.
I love you—
and all our adventures together,
the laughter, the quiet moments,
the lessons, the stories,
And the love that weaves through it all.
Forever,
I carry you with me,
And I know that no matter where life leads,
your heart will always be my home.

10 ONCE BLUE

Back when these floors were blue,
Where the creaks and moans hid away.
The walls changed color over the years,
And the house remains sturdy and strong.
A shelter and a home.
Halls that echoed children's laughter,
Their footsteps are light and full of wonder.
Rooms that once held the hum of
conversation,
the clatter of dishes,
The gentle rhythm of life unfolding day by
day.
The sunlight would spill through the
windows in the late afternoon,
Casting golden patterns across those blue
floors.
Even as the paint faded and the walls
shifted shades,
Something deeper remained—
the spirit of the place,
The warmth that never left.
For within these walls,
Time may have marched on,
But the memories stayed,

woven into the grain of the wood,
the laughter still whispering softly
Beneath the echo of every step.

11 FAMILIAR SOUNDS

The hum of air compressors and machinery—
Familiar sounds.
The metal and tin shakes and compressor buildings,
The sounds of the trade.
Yet also the sounds of childhood,
In oil and gas, it's as familiar as breathing.
A dark blue fanny pack filled with tools, a helping hand,
And a steady aim with the flashlight.
The air was thick with the scent of grease and earth,
And the steady thrum of engines was like a heartbeat—
Constant, grounding, alive.
Each clang and echo was a note in the song of the day,
A rhythm learned young,
Woven into memory.
There was pride in those sounds,
A quiet knowing that work was being done,
That something was built, repaired, or kept alive.

And through it all,
the blue fanny pack and the flashlight's
glow
stood as quiet reminders—
of helping hands,
of shared moments,
And of a bond forged in the hum of work
and love.

12 BLUE COVERALLS

Blue coveralls and yellow safety stripes.
Hard hats and Tic Tacs and beef jerky.
Oil stains.
Ice fishing and lost soup ladles.
All small pieces of a life built by hand—
the smell of diesel and cold metal,
The way the frost clung to windows in early morning light.
The laughter that echoed through job sites and over frozen lakes,
Where work and play blurred together in the rhythm of everyday living.
There's something familiar in it all—
the rustle of coveralls,
the jingle of keys,
The quiet hum of a truck cooling down after a long day.
Memories stitched together with grit and warmth,
with hard work and small joys—
the comfort of jerky in a pocket,
the sweetness of a mint,
The laughter over a soup ladle gone missing beneath the ice.

Simple things,
But they linger—
fragments of home,
of family,
Of a life both ordinary and beautiful.

13 TEACUPS

Teacups and tea.
I don't remember when I first fell in love
with a teacup.
I do remember my first tea set—one of
them anyway.
I recall several sets over the years, plastic
ones that I had,
But when I became particular, it was the
little glass set that my great-grandma Becky
gave to me.
I believe it was for Christmas.
It's tucked away, safe and sound now
that I'm grown up.
I have many teacups.
I grew up with tea parties—
with biscuits and cookies, splendid tea,
tea parties with dolls,
tea parties with my mom,
And tea parties with my grandma.
Even though I still prefer tea over coffee,
I like to drink it in fancy teacups.
My tea collection continues to grow,
each cup holding not just tea,
but memories of laughter, warmth, and the

quiet joy of sitting together,
of moments both ordinary and magical,
Woven into the rims and patterns of each
delicate vessel.

14 HARD WORK

I grew up in the oil and gas field.
A wrench in my hand and a hard hat upon my head.

Ice fishing and lost soup ladles.
I grew up with my parents saying that hard work is hard work, no matter the work, and that no work or job should ever be looked down upon. A job puts food on the table and pays the bills. Sometimes, we love the jobs we have, and other times, they are just to make ends meet.

There will be times when there is sacrifice, and bills and money are tight.
I learned that experiences are worth more than all the latest gadgets and that one can do a lot with sticks and imagination.

I learned to read instruction manuals, and that while most things can be fixed and repaired, some are better replaced.
While I have all brothers, if there was a leaky sink there, I'd be there with my plastic bucket and screwdriver, ready to attempt my hand at plumbing.

I was taught to be independent, to ask

for help, and to admit when I didn't know something.
I learned to take pride in what I could do and humility in what I could not.
I learned that work was not just a task—it was a way to care for oneself, for family, for the life being built around you.
And in the oil and gas fields, with wrenches, hard hats, and ice fishing adventures, I learned that life, like machinery, sometimes needs patience, attention, and the willingness to get your hands dirty.

15 THE VALLEY

Growing up in the county of Athabasca, the rolling hills and valleys of Athabasca, Athabasca flowing through a place that would be home to her.

When one thinks of history, it's the places and people of the past that shape the future. Their stories and their work made an impact.

One thinks of the pioneers, the ones who blazed trails, those with curious minds of discovery.

I grew up with stories of a town rich and full of history and possibilities. Farmers and coal miners, loggers and the great logs that came floating down the Athabasca River. Stories of the ice bridges and when the first bridge was built, of the ferry boat rides. Stories of the great fire and how it changed the direction and course of the town.

In our lives, there are stories, people, and moments all wrapped up together. Our lives are like quilts sewn together. Sometimes, the stitches are straight; sometimes, they're a little wobbly and shaky. Other times, we have patchwork quilts, mismatched tiles, and thatch fabrics. Together, lives are like a great quilt. Living and breathing are woven together over time, imprinted and fused within the colors, memories, and moments where others have touched our lives.

A quilt—a story, a moment in time.

Some quilts, I was told, you knew the story about them right away.

For others, it takes time to reveal their story; it's like a quilter putting together their quilt.

They start with their blocks and cutting, making each piece, piecing them together, stitching, sewing, steaming, and pressing them all together—just as our lives are layered.

As a child, I grew up with quilts: quilted walls, hangings, pillows, blankets, and the stories they all carried.

I watched as my mother sewed in the night or prepared so well that we went to bed.

I think of past generations and the history behind sewing and quilting, how it is passed down from one generation to the next.

How, in the past, it was such a necessity —part of survival —a skill that meant more when society was less materialistic, less automatic, and more manual. Things meant more when you worked for them.

Just as quilts have their own story, we, too, have our own stories that mingle.

A quilt is like a storybook, only its story isn't hidden in pages—it is spread out wide for all to see.

Bright and vibrant colors, patterns, and shapes, secrets discovered, hidden whispers of a crafter.

The gift of a quilt: warm on a winter night, comfort when one is sick. Loving hands, stitching together, matching and placing squares and triangles, hexagons, modeling through this match—colors faded, colors bright, doll colors.

And yet the doll colors were never fully dull, because they were always stitched together too—a beautiful masterpiece, the words of life pressed into every story it could tell.

16 STITCHES OF A LIFE

Knitted together
with the words of one's heart and soul,
the patterns and loops of one's life story
all strong together,
Held at the seams with words and stitches.
Our stories have been made into a quilt.
Oh, how they would be—
intricate designs and patterns,
How colors and threads would change
Along with the seasons of one's life.

17 JULY 19, 2017

I wonder about the future, and I wonder how different things will shape the rest of my life. I know I will use and learn different things off and on, and some will continue to be used for their last night. I wonder about the friendships I'll make. I think about the ones I have made and how summer will go by, and will carry me with it. It will pass in a blur. I think about the people I can count on my fingers, the ones that go past finger counting and past using my toes to count, so much so that I have to do math. I think of those who've watched me grow and aided me. I think of the people who have inspired me. Life is such a wonderful gift, and I'm so blessed for all the people who have made a difference in my life. Many people have walked with me and journeyed with me, while some are gone, and summer remains, and some have trusted away in my heart; each day remains.

18 CATCHING STARS

She stood back, taking it all in—hours,
minutes, and years of writing—how it grew
and the way it all fit together.
The story shared, the start of a project, the
books lined up on the shelf, all by her.
Sometimes wishes are dreams that seem
as though we are trying to catch shooting
stars.
Yet most great things we start have begun
with an idea, a spark, and a dream.
Dreams can become reality.
She thinks of her younger self and
recognizes that she had done it—
She had caught the stars of dreams.
She was an author, and her books could be
shared.
She'd grown to let the words fly free,
To let the reader see all that lay behind her
dark eyes.
And the long dream of authorhood and
girlhood.

19 WITHIN US

It can be found in the little moments,
in the little things—
Things that spark memory,
Things we don't realize carry with us,
Bits and pieces of things that shape us,
Of others that have clung to us
And may become our own.
That smell of the laundry detergent from
that trip,
stuffed in the back,
not worn since the summer vacation—
that smell of sunshine and ocean,
That bit of peace that clings to us.
The mannerisms we have,
The way we move our hands,
How we talk,
How we cook things,
How we do things—
It comes from generations,
It comes from friends and family,
Things we pick up,
Things that stay.
All of it stitched quietly into us,
woven through years and moments,

Carried without knowing.
And in these small, familiar ways,
We are never entirely our own—
We are a beautiful gathering.
Of everyone we have ever loved.

20 WOVEN WORDS

Words, a friend in form, are beautiful and cruel.
They are threads of thought spun from the soul,
Woven into sentences that can comfort or destroy.
Words on their own can be simply that—
soft syllables, quiet whispers waiting to be shaped—
But it's people who place them and utter them,
Who uses them wisely or unwisely,
Those who misuse or mistreat words.
A single word can build a bridge or burn one down.
It can be a balm or a blade,
A spark that lights a dream or one that sets it aflame.
People can be dangerous when their words are thrown about,
When they forget the power they hold,
And one doesn't stop to see if it was just or wise.
Harshness and anger spoil words in their

beauty,
Turning poetry to ash and song to silence.
Crumbling people as they destroy,
They trample hearts and steal the soul,
leaving behind the echoes of things once spoken—
Words that can never be taken back,
Only remembered in the hollow quiet after.
Yet even then, words can heal.
They can rise again from the ruins,
Gentle as morning light after the longest night.
For though they wound, they also mend,
and within their fragile beauty,
There is always the chance.
To begin again.

21 POTTERY

Hands in clay.
Mud pressed between fingers.
The wheel turns and turns, slow and steady. Generations in the hands before you, in the hands beside you, Stories pressed into every curve.
The clay remembers.
It holds the echoes of voices, of hands shaping, molding, lifting, Hands that made, that loved, that lived.
Each pot, each bowl,
Each little vessel— a story kept, a memory carried, passed down from hand to hand, from mud to fire to life.
The kiln breathes,
And the clay hardens.
Yet the stories remain, in the cracks, the curves, the smooth and the rough, quietly waiting to be touched again.

22 STITCHED DAYS

Days and times
stitch together,
It seemed all complete,
Complicated and convoluted.
One step here,
one step back,
Always so much more to be done.
Thoughts exploring,
wiggling around,
Oh, how backwards and disorganized
It could be—
Yet within the chaos,
There is movement,
a rhythm,
a weaving of moments
that slowly, quietly
Becomes the story of a life.

23 CASTING WORDS TO THE SEA

I've cast my heart out upon the pages,
throwing my net into the sea,
Waiting with bated breath for what would come next.
Each word, a ripple upon the water,
Each sentence is a fragile hope drifting into the unknown.
Oh, how this writer's soul could feel a little heavy at times,
burdened by the weight of emotion and memory,
Of stories that demanded to be told,
Even when they clawed their way out in fragments and sighs.
How some words were too painful or irksome to write,
How they caught in the throat before spilling across the page.
It's been an endeavor—
a journey of soul-searching and surrender,
Of gathering courage from the quiet corners of the heart.
The truth was tumbling in words and

sentences strung together,
imperfect but honest,
Stitched with the trembling hands of one
who dared to feel.
It was not a path for the faint of heart.
To write was to open every door long
locked,
to let the tide rush in,
To drown and rise again within one's own
creation.
For every page is both a wound and a
healing,
A confession and a song.
And still, I keep casting my net—
hoping that somewhere out there,
Someone will catch what I've set free.

24 WORDS WERE EVERYWHERE

Words were everywhere.
The writer looked—
Signs, labels, spoken and read—
They danced in song, every which way.
They were loud and bold,
Quiet, whispered, and traded.
Words are a powerful thing,
A commodity, a source of trade.
The world revolves around words—
What people say, shout, and phrase.
They were painted across walls,
etched into paper,
And carried in the wind between
conversations.
Some fell gently like raindrops,
Others struck like thunder,
Shaping hearts and histories alike.
The writer watched,
collecting them like scattered stars,
each one holding a meaning,
A secret, a story of its own.
For words could build bridges or burn them,
Heal wounds or reopen them,

Bring people closer or tear them apart.
And still, she loved them—
The weight, the wonder, the wildness of words.
For in the end,
It was through them
That the world continued to spin,
And that she found her place within it.

25 WORDS AND QUILTS

Words are crafted, honed,
strung and stitched together,
Pressed into the seams.
Books and stories are like quilts—
their spines bound,
at times worn
And in need of mending.
Each page is a patch,
each phrase a thread,
Woven with care and memory.
They warm the soul
on the coldest nights,
reminding us that even
in frayed edges and faded ink,
There is beauty—
A life pieced together.
Through words that endure.

26 THE KEEPER OF SECRETS

Words whispered to the soul.
The keeper of secrets was hungry.
Its teeth gnashed and were gnawed,
They were exchanged and tumbled about.
There was always a price to pay
to have the weight of one's secrets
Given to another.
It fed on the tremble of confession,
on the hush between breaths—
a hunger not for flesh,
But for truth,
For the taste of what was hidden.
And once spoken,
The words no longer belonged.
To the one who uttered them—
They belonged to the keeper,
To the silence that followed,
To the dark corners where secrets sleep.

27 THE WRITER ON THE ROAD

The writer was used to the long hours.
and the whirling hum of compressors,
Insights murmuring in the background.
She took hold of the waiting moments,
Stitched together and strung words across the page.
Some days there was more or less waiting—
Some days, the author scarcely picked up the pen,
For life was busy,
the hours filled with driving,
And the company of one's own thoughts.
The words itched to get out,
To tumble onto paper.
The air was filled with stories,
podcasts, music, and song—
and sometimes,
the silence itself,
filtered only by the low rumble,
The hum of the engine sounds.
The passage of time and hours melted into each other.
Each passing kilometer

added, recalculated,
counted out in the glow of gas station lights—
always forward and onward,
the road unrolling ahead,
The wind whispers:
Forward, forward, and on.

28 LOVER OF BOOKS

There she was,
a lover of books,
finding herself tucked away,
A book never far from hand.
Time flipped and filled.
with the turning of pages,
each page a doorway,
Each word is a step into another world.
Time can be spent in many ways,
But reading never goes wrong.
Well, it can be backwards.
and confusing at times,
as a dyslexic,
Yet the world within books
It is endlessly amazing to explore.
There is so much
That can be discovered,
so many stories to wander through,
so many voices whispering from the past,
so many worlds waiting patiently,
their secrets tucked in between lines,
Their magic is alive in the quiet of a turning page.
And she drifts there,

Lost and found all at once,
wrapped in the wonder of stories,
Where imagination stretches like sunlight
across the years of her life,
and the love of books
Becomes a lifelong home.

29 ESCAPES INTO BOOKS

She picked up another book,
if only to disappear,
to forget,
Even for just a little while.
She had been escaping into books.
for a really long time—
They were her other worlds,
her secret places,
Where she could let her worries wait,
And stories unravel
Before her eyes.
Each page offered a doorway,
each word a gentle escape,
a chance to breathe
And wander far from the weight.
Of the world outside.
In the quiet of turning pages,
She found herself,
Lost and found again,
carried away
by the endless magic
Of stories waiting to be discovered.

30 STITCHED

They were all stitched up in me—
little things,
these moments,
these glimpses of people and mannerisms,
The way in which one moves,
The way in which one thinks.
Sometimes recipes are passed down
through generations,
Or the way in which your friend made
something
or did something—
And it stays with us.
We stitch it all together,
each fragment a thread,
Each memory is a patch in the quilt of who
we are.
Oh, how delightful,
How lovely,
That we are made of so many others—
woven of laughter,
of stories shared across tables,
of gestures remembered,
And of kindnesses tucked quietly into the
folds of our hearts.

31 WEARY

The writer was weary.
The cold made her ache,
And she felt dreary
Every which way to Sunday.
It's hard—
bouncing through life,
Living with chronic health issues and pain.
There's only so much one can do,
Only so many spoons to give,
And yet each day demands more,
pulling at the edges
of energy, of hope,
Of spirit.
Even in the ache,
She keeps moving,
writing, breathing,
finding small moments
That reminds her
There is still light.
Amid the heaviness.

32 SECRETS IN THE PAGES

Do you know the secrets?
Tucked away within the pages of books?
What the scrolls say,
What do the stories whisper?
Words and books are powerful.
They lead to many things.
They leave a hole within,
a longing, a lost piece,
Surely the reason
The Alexandria Royal Library was burned—
too much power,
too much knowledge
Contained within those walls.
It was written within the pages.
The parts of her were tucked away.
for safekeeping,
kept until the time
to collect them,
to put herself back together,
piece by piece,
Story by story.

33 THE TEA CABINET

There it was in the corner—
a light brown painted cabinet,
a China cabinet lined inside
with tiled multicolored shelves,
filled with teacups and teapots
And things related to tea.
Oh, how lovely it is to see—
The lover of tea found great joy.
in that little cabinet.
Everything had its place,
Everything sat just right.
How marvelous it is,
How beautiful teatime can be—
a pause in the day,
a comfort of clinking porcelain,
the soft steam rising,
The world is slowing down.
To sip a moment of calm.

34 PURPOSE IN WRITING

I've been thinking of the future,
The direction of my purpose.
As I continue to write books,
to write down these different things in my life,
I see where God is leading me.
And the possibilities unfold.
I think of the ways God can use my writing.
to help others, to inspire,
To bring them closer to Him.
I think of the opportunities.
to meet people,
to encourage hearts,
To guide them gently toward hope and light.
Even if it's not millions of people,
Even if it's only a handful,
If just a few read my words
And find comfort,
understanding,
Or a spark of faith, then God has used me.
as His instrument,
And my purpose is alive.

35 CHOSEN FAMILY

Life can be strange sometimes.
At times, we can be so close to people,
And other times, we drift apart.
Yet some things tether our souls deeply to others,
so that no matter the time or the distance,
Those people always remain.
You can pick up right where you left off,
As though no time at all has passed.
In reality, it's been a long time.
Those people are few and far between,
So those friendships and relationships should be cherished.
It is a blessing to have friends,
And a blessing to have those who are not family by blood,
yet chosen family,
That no matter what, you know they have your back.
Sometimes, chosen family.
It is better than blood family.

36 THE IMPACT OF WORDS

I wonder how my writing is.
Can impact others.
I know I have to buy my books,
But you never really get to hear.
All the feedback from those books.
If it's friends or family,
Yes, you can hear some back,
but strangers—
strangers buying your book,
Sometimes you never hear from them.
Other times,
You happen to meet that one person.
Who sees the book
And recognizes the beauty of it.
The opportunity for them
to draw closer to God
through your work, through your words—
That is why I write.
I think that's really what I set out to do:
to put together these tangible moments in my life
And share them with others.

37 REFLECTIONS OF TIME

It was an interesting time,
a time filled with reflection,
pondering the past,
moments of relationships
And those who matter most.
As one curates their guest list for an
important event,
such as a wedding,
One thinks of those who have made an
impact on their life,
Those who have brought joy,
and those who, no matter what,
Have always supported you.
No matter the time that goes by,
or the distance,
There are some people
who, no matter what,
You know you can count on.
You know you can pick up the phone,
And they'll be there to help you along.
Sometimes it's easy to forget that those
people are there.
Sometimes we drift apart.
And yet, at times,

They're just a knock away,
a phone call away,
An outstretched hand away.
Sometimes all we need to do is ask.
Sometimes we forget.
Sometimes distance feels so far,
And yet, a sadness fills the heart
For times once passed.
And yet, sometimes, things can go back
the way they were,
And other times, they cannot.
Life is like an hourglass.
It goes up, it goes down,
and is filled with unexpected things—
little treasures and moments,
All that adds up like the grains of sand,
time slipping through our hands,
time all around us,
like the beating of a heart,
not always seen,
But always felt.

ABOUT THE AUTHOR

Ruby F. Nazaruk lives in rural Alberta with her husband. A lifelong storyteller, she has spent her days surrounded by words — writing, reading, and sharing the stories that shape the heart of everyday life. From a young age, Ruby found magic in books and the power of imagination, a spark that continues to guide her creative journey.

She writes with the hope that her stories will inspire others to dream boldly, to put pen to paper, and to follow the quiet callings of their own hearts.

www.ingramcontent.com/pod-product-compliance
Lightning Source LLC
LaVergne TN
LVHW020657100826
845148LV00012B/2529

* 9 7 8 1 7 3 8 3 5 9 0 4 2 *